No. 36 Grenade

Home Guard Instruction

The Naval & Military Press Ltd

Published by the
The Naval & Military Press
in association with the Royal Armouries

Unit 10 Ridgewood Industrial Park,
Uckfield, East Sussex, TN22 5QE
Tel: +44 (0) 1825 749494
Fax: +44 (0) 1825 765701

MILITARY HISTORY AT YOUR FINGERTIPS
www.naval-military-press.com

ONLINE GENEALOGY RESEARCH
www.military-genealogy.com

ONLINE MILITARY CARTOGRAPHY
www.militarymaproom.com

ROYAL ARMOURIES

The Library & Archives Department at the Royal Armouries Museum, Leeds, specialises in the history and development of armour and weapons from earliest times to the present day. Material relating to the development of artillery and modern fortifications is held at the Royal Armouries Museum, Fort Nelson.

For further information contact:
Royal Armouries Museum, Library, Armouries Drive,
Leeds, West Yorkshire LS10 1LT
Royal Armouries, Library, Fort Nelson, Down End Road, Fareham PO17 6AN

Or visit the Museum's website at
www.armouries.org.uk

Printed and bound by CPI Antony Rowe, Eastbourne

WEST RIDING ZONE.

No. 36 Grenade.

INSTRUCTION.

CONFIDENTIAL.

The following lectures, information, and diagrams of apparatus, have been extracted from :—

S. A. T. Vol. i, Pamphlet No. 13. 1937.
S. A. T. Vol. V. 1931.

The drawings of the throwing positions have been approved by the I. T. C. Weapon Training Officers in the W.R. Area.

The standard set is high, but can easily be attained by practice.

FOREWORD.

ONE of the greatest difficulties so far as the Home Guard officer and N.C.O. is concerned is the fact that he is also a civilian, who, in most cases, is already, quite apart from his military duties, working, and working very long hours, at his civil avocation. This leaves him with but limited time at his disposal for the rest of the day. He is often, in the beginning, out of touch with modern military developments and has, therefore, to strike a balance between the time he can spare to read his military literature, of which necessity there is always a spate in wartime, and the time he can spend in practical training himself and in the training of his men; unfortunately the two go hand in hand and each is complementary to the other. Then, too, information about any particular subject, if it is to be complete, has often to be searched for in two or more pamphlets, supplemented by notes taken on courses, and so on. Anything, therefore, which collects together in one cover the information from all sources and puts it in a terse, clear and abbreviated manner, is of the utmost value in these particular circumstances.

Lt.-Col. Knights-Trench is the Yorkshire Area Bombing and Explosives Officer. He likes grenades; he treats them as his pets, or rather, perhaps, as I treat my camera; an ingenious device, full of interest, requiring knowledge to get the best out of it, and worth while taking a little trouble to know properly. A bombing enthusiast can be something of a menace; we all know the man in the Great War who used to take the pin out of a Mills in a dug-out just to show "how it was done," but enthusiasm of the sort which Lt.-Col. Knights-Trench displays can be productive of nothing but good. His book contains little that is new, but, as far as I am aware, it is new in the sense that it has concentrated all the available information on the Mills Grenade in one cover and in a readable accessible form. It cannot fail to be of use to members of the Home Guard in teaching them how to get the best out of that very important weapon, the Mills Grenade.

19 Blake Street,
York.
14th July, 1941.

Col.
G.S.O.I. H.G.
Yorkshire Area.

2

LECTURE ON No. 36 H.E. GRENADE
(to be elaborated).

The No. 36 Grenade, when thrown, is essentially a close-range weapon, and is of the greatest importance to the Home-Guard. In fact, it is their personal weapon. It can be thrown a distance of from 25-35 yards—although some will improve upon this. Accuracy of aim is, however, more important than distance. The Grenade has a danger area of 25-30 yards in all directions from point of burst. In actual fact it is capable of inflicting a wound up to 300 yards from point of burst, particularly if it explodes on hard ground. The possibility of ricochet of fragments must also be reckoned with according to the conditions of the area where thrown.

In the extended style of fighting the H.G. may be called upon to do, in which operations may be carried out in small groups or parties against an enemy behind cover or in moving vehicles such as cars, lorries, etc., and on account of the speed of movement to-day, when a distant enemy may rapidly come within close range, the No. 36 is invaluable. A good example is the clearing of houses in which the enemy may have taken up position. It is also excellent as a surprise weapon, and in street fighting.

The weight of the Grenade is about 1½ lbs., and the method of delivery is described as "throwing," though it is really "overarm lobbing"—that is, it must have a high trajectory in flight with a steep angle of descent.

The value of this is that an enemy who may be behind bullet-proof cover can be bombed and driven out into the open.

Also the steep descent results in the bomb remaining on or near to the spot at which it is aimed instead of continuing to roll forward, as would be the case if thrown flat. The importance of this is obvious when throwing on to or in the track of moving vehicles.

The Service Pattern No. 36 Grenade is varnished blackish-brown in colour. It has a green band round the centre of body, and three red crosses on either side of filling screw. These markings denote that it is filled with H.E. Grenades may still be seen with a red band round the top, passing over filling screw. This also denotes "filled," but with different H.E. The dummy Grenade is grey or may be painted white—no band.

(The first and most important rule whenever you are given a live Grenade is to apply the "first-safety precaution." Unscrew the base plug, holding the Grenade base uppermost, and look to see if it is primed—i.e., contains its detonator, or igniter set.)

3

DESCRIPTION OF PARTS

(using cut Grenade and diagram No. 1.)

1. Body :—Cast iron.

Serrated to promote fragmentation and give good grip. Two shoulders grooved to carry and locate trunnions on striker lever. Hole in top for striker pin. Small holes in shoulders for safety pin.

Recess for lever—must be flush fitting

(*important—see under* "examination").

Screwed filling hole.

Centre piece :—

Two sleeves.

Large for striker and spring.

Small for detonator.

Makes gas-tight joint with lead washer inside top of body.

Base Plug :—

Covers centre piece and holds igniter set in position.

Has two recesses for key and a screwed centre hole for gas check. This last is for firing from the Northover Projector.

Striker Group :—

The striker has a slot in the neck to receive the striker lever when spring is compressed.

Base of striker has a rim which holds the spring under compression between itself and the inside of the body. On the face of the striker base there are two nipples and a slot which forms a gas escape. The spring fits round the striker. The striker lever has trunnions which fit in the grooves on the shoulders. One end of the lever engages in striker slot. The remainder lies flush in recess in body, behind the shoulders.

The lever is held in position by safety pin which passes over the lever through holes in the shoulders.

Igniter Set :—

Composed of a cap chamber fitted with a ·22 rim fire cartridge case provided with a central gas escape which should be covered with waxed paper disc to exclude damp.

A fuse is fitted into the cartridge case, and the joint is varnished. The other end of the fuse is crimped or nipped into a detonator, and the joint luted.

4

Note.—If the fuse is buff coloured it burns for 7 seconds; if white, for 4 seconds. (The latter has small rubber band on fuse to help recognition in the dark.)

The detonator contains a fulminating substance and is extremely sensitive. The set, therefore, should always be handled with care, and held only by the cap chamber and fuse. The detonator should never be knocked, damaged or subjected to heat or friction.

The action or mechanism :—(Demonstrate with cut Grenade.)

When the safety pin is removed and bomb is thrown, the lever on leaving the hand flies off, and the striker thus released is forced downwards under the impulse of the spring. The nipples on striking the rim of the cartridge cap cause a flash which starts the fuse burning. The fuse burns for 7 or 4 seconds, as the case may be, and then fires the detonator which, in its turn, detonates the H.E., causing the Grenade to explode. The gases from the burning fuse escape through the central escape in the cap chamber, and thence through the slot n base of striker and so via the sleeve to the outside of the bomb.

Treat all bombs as having 4-seconds fuses.

Hand Grenade, N° 36, Mark I

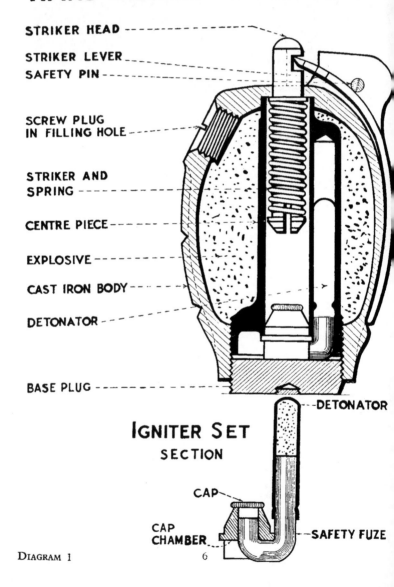

STRIKER HEAD

STRIKER LEVER

SAFETY PIN

SCREW PLUG
IN FILLING HOLE

STRIKER AND
SPRING

CENTRE PIECE

EXPLOSIVE

CAST IRON BODY

DETONATOR

BASE PLUG

DETONATOR

Igniter Set
SECTION

CAP

CAP
CHAMBER

SAFETY FUZE

Diagram 1

6

Examination and Priming.

The Grenades are delivered into stores assembled and ready filled (coloured band), but unprimed. The igniter sets are contained in a separate box on the lid of which is clearly indicated what they are, and the burning time of the fuse they contain—this may be 4 or 7 seconds —indicated, as explained, by the colour.

As you may be given the work of priming the Grenades prior to action, it is necessary that you should know how to make an examination before priming for faults and defects.

First of all, apply the safety precaution of making certain that the Grenade is not primed.

External Examination.

(*a*) Examine the outside of the body for cracks through which damp might enter into the H.E., causing a blind.

(*b*) Examine the filling screw to see that it is screwed up tight and sealed to keep out damp.

(*c*) Examine the body shoulders to see that they are sound and un-broken, so that no premature release of the striker can occur.

(*d*) See that the point where the striker projects through the top of the body has been properly sealed with luting to keep damp out of the centre piece. See also that the lever is properly engaged in the striker slot.

(*e*) Examine safety pin to see that it is sound and that the lever is properly held by it in the shoulders. The lever should lie close to the Grenade so that it cannot catch in the ring of another Grenade.

Internal Examination.

The Grenade must first be stripped as follows :—

Close the points of the safety pin and, holding the lever against the Grenade, withdraw the pin. Next hold the base of the bomb against the body and release lever allowing the striker to fall. Remove striker and spring.

(*a*) Take striker from spring, and examine base for nipples and gas slot. A Grenade in which the spring appears to be weak should not be used. Test freedom of striker movement by replacing without spring and moving up and down in striker hole.

Clean all parts thoroughly free from grease.

(*b*) Examine the centre piece as carefully as possible, looking for corrosion and cracks in the wall between the two sleeves which would allow the flash from the cap to pass direct to the detonator and might cause a premature burst. **The centre piece is never removed.** See that there is no grit in centre sleeve, or obstruction in detonator sleeve. (A.C.I. No. 241 of February 4th, 1942 states Grenades with these faults may be used.)

To assemble the Grenade after examination, replace striker and spring, and with a dummy cartridge force the striker through the top of the Grenade and engage the striker lever in the striker slot. Press striker lever down against the body, and replace the safety pin from right to left when holding the Grenade with the lever to the front and the filling screw towards you. Open out the points slightly to secure the pin.

Examination of Igniter Set.

This is always done before priming the Grenade. The set should be held by the cap chamber and fuse, and treated gently. **The igniter set is never dismantled.**

(*a*) Inspect central gas escape to see that it is covered with water-proof paper to prevent damp. Igniter set not rejected if absent.

(*b*) See that the fuse is firmly fixed to the cap chamber and the joint varnished.

(*c*) Examine the detonator to make sure that it is firmly crimped or nipped on to the fuse, and that the joint is luted to exclude the possibility of a flash passing direct to the detonator. "Luting" is not essential under war conditions.

If the examination brings any fault or defect to light, reject the Grenade or igniter set. Do not prime.

Priming the Grenade.

Hold the igniter set in the right hand, thumb on the cap chamber and forefinger on the outside portion of the fuse. Press both together firmly. (This ensures that the cap chamber and detonator are correctly aligned for entry into their respective sleeves.) Holding the set in the manner explained, slide the detonator into its sleeve, gradually removing the forefinger, but retaining the pressure of the thumb until the cap chamber is almost home, now press the cap chamber fully home. Replace base plug, and tighten up with key.

THROWING INSTRUCTION.

It is not possible for the average man to "throw" a Grenade weighing $1\frac{1}{2}$ lbs. Moreover, to obtain maximum effectiveness, it is necessary to impart a high angle of flight so as to get a steep angle of descent. The action, therefore, is an overarm swing or lob.

Accuracy is much more important than distance. There is no advantage in being able to send a Grenade a long way if the direction is wide of the target.

Distance is dependent upon the development of a free, natural swing and plenty of practice throwing with dummies.

After a preliminary instruction in the general principles of "throwing" a man should be allowed to "throw" in the way most natural to him. If this enables him to obtain the distance and accuracy of aim required, he should not be worried on small details of style, provided that he conforms generally to the methods further described.

On their first visit to a bombing range the men should first practice the over-arm swing—in shirt sleeves if desired. Service conditions of dress will be necessary as they progress, including steel helmet.

When they show a good swing and fair accuracy, then practice with dummy Grenades should be commenced as follows :—

1. Standing position :—

    (a) Throw over 18-ft. high wire 15 yards from throwing base into pit 25 yards from base.

        This teaches the men to obtain a high trajectory and steep angle of descent—as explained on page 1. (See diagram No. 2.)

    (b) Throw from cage (diagram No. 3). This teaches a combination of length and direction with high throwing from cover. It gives "throwing control."

2. Lying or Prone Position :—

    The men will throw from behind low cover over the high wire into pits arranged as described in 1 (a).

Note.—If permanent cages are not available, the arrangements shown in diagram may be marked out with flags or sandbags. A good substitute for the high wire is goal posts provided that they give the 18-ft. height required.

Other types of practice range for variation of direction and distance are shown in diagrams 4, 5 and 6.

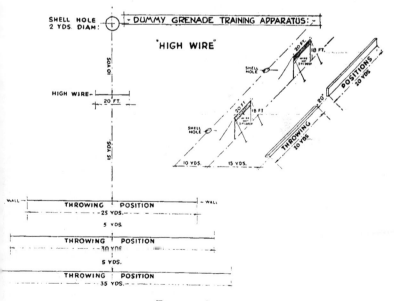

DIAGRAM 2

9

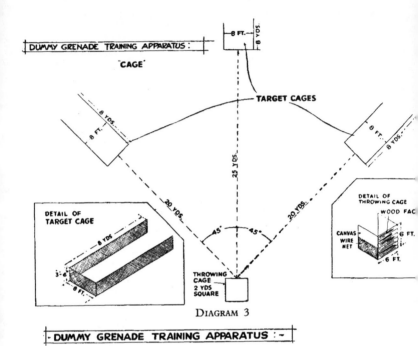

DIAGRAM 3

- DUMMY GRENADE TRAINING APPARATUS : -

FIG. 1. "SHELL HOLE"

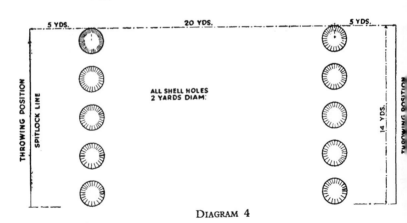

DIAGRAM 4

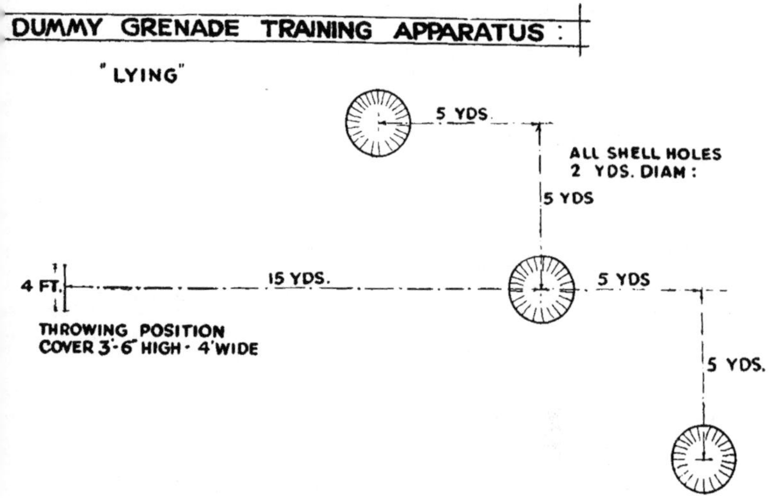

DUMMY GRENADE TRAINING APPARATUS :

"LYING"

5 YDS.

ALL SHELL HOLES
2 YDS. DIAM :

5 YDS

4 FT. — — — 15 YDS. — — — 5 YDS.

THROWING POSITION
COVER 3'-6" HIGH · 4'WIDE

5 YDS.

DIAGRAM 5

~DUMMY GRENADE TRAINING APPARATUS :~

"CONE"

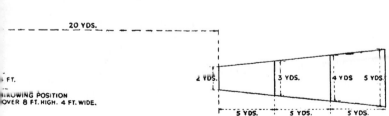

20 YDS.

FT.

THROWING POSITION
OVER 8 FT. HIGH. 4 FT. WIDE.

2 YDS.   3 YDS.   4 YDS   5 YDS

5 YDS.   5 YDS.   5 YDS.

DIAGRAM 6

Details of Standing Positions :—

This position is used when throwing from a trench or from behind cover varying from 4 feet 6 inches to 6 feet. The actual position may therefore be erect or semi-erect.

Demonstrate and explain the several movements as follows :—
(using diagrams   ).

1. Ready : (diagram 7).

Stand sideways to the target, the feet placed well apart and square to the direction of throw. Hold the Grenade in the right hand with the striker lever under the second joint of the fingers and the thumb passing over or just below the filling screw. Grip the Grenade firmly, with the knuckles of the hand uppermost, and the wrist resting against the waist or right thigh according to whether an erect or semi-erect position is necessary.

If erect, the weight of the body may be distributed evenly on both feet. If semi-erect, a partial crouch is necessary with the weight on the rear foot.

The first or second finger of the left hand should grip the safety pin firmly.

DIAGRAM 7

12

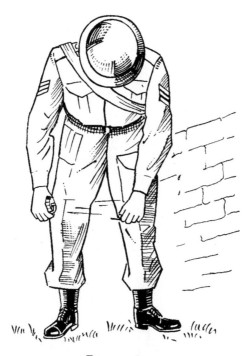

DIAGRAM 8

2. Prepare to Throw (diagrams 8 and 9).

Keep the left arm still and close to the body. Withdraw the pin—
in practice go through this action—by thrusting the right hand slightly
downwards and backwards. Before carrying the hand to the rear for
throwing, inspect the Grenade shoulders to ensure that the whole
pin has been removed. The pin must be retained on the finger until
the Grenade has been thrown.

3. Throw (diagram 10).

The bomber should now have naturally assumed the correct position
for throwing, that is, eyes fixed on or in direction of the target, keeping the left shoulder pointing at the target. Slightly bend the knees.
Swing back as far as possible, allowing the left arm (and foot if necessary)
to come up naturally. Without a pause swing quickly forward, keeping the right arm extended and deliver the Grenade. During this
movement the weight should naturally be transferred from the right
to the left foot.

DIAGRAM 9

The men should first practice the throwing action without Grenades.

The instructor should then supervise the throwing of four dummy Grenades by each man.

Conditions of test :—

4 out of 6 Grenades should fall inside a 10-ft. diameter circle 25 yards from throwing base, passing over an 18-ft. high wire 15 yards from the base, and 10 yards from the circle.

Details of Lying or Prone Position :—

Where only low cover is available, it will be necessary to throw the Grenade from a prone position, and it is important that the movements required for throwing from this position should be practised so that the throwing attitude is obtained, the Grenade thrown, and cover regained in the shortest possible time, and with the least effort.

14

DIAGRAM 10

Demonstrate and explain the several movements as follows :—
(using diagrams 11—16).

1. Ready.

Lie face downwards directly in line with the target, holding the Grenade as in the standing position, with both hands just in front of the face and with elbows outwards.

15

DIAGRAM 11

2. Prepare to Throw : (diagram 11).
Pull the bomb away from the pin, just sufficiently to ensure that the whole pin is removed. Glance at the shoulders to see that this is so. The pin should be retained on the finger until the Grenade has been thrown.

3. Throw : (diagrams 12—16).

Gripping the bomb and bomb lever firmly in the right hand, and the safety pin in the left hand, place the hands on the ground slightly in rear of the shoulder blades and close to the body (diagram 12). Press quickly upwards. Keeping the left knee on the ground, swing the body quickly back, allowing the right leg and foot to go well back in a straight line, but naturally (diagram 13). At the same time—keeping the eyes and left shoulder on the line of the target—continue the backward swing, carrying the right hand to the rear and allowing the left arm to come up (diagram 14).

Swing forward, keeping the right arm extended and using the thrust of the right leg to give added momentum (diagram 15). Deliver the Grenade, observe its direction of flight, and quickly lie down behind cover, placing the hands over the base of the skull (diagram 16).

The men should first practice the throwing action without Grenades, after which the instructor will supervise each man in turn throwing 4 Grenades over the high wire.

DIAGRAM 12

DIAGRAM 13

DIAGRAM 14

17

DIAGRAM 15

DIAGRAM 16

Tests of elementary training :—

1. Mechanism, care and cleaning.

Total of four questions covering the subjects stated below will be asked, and satisfactory knowledge in three out of the four must be shown.

    (*a*) The mechanism and action of the No. 36 Grenade.

    (*b*) Examination of Grenades and detonators—priming.

Each man will be required to carry out the tests with dummy material, describing at the same time what he is doing.

    (*c*) Throwing.

This test will be carried out from behind standing cover over the high wire into a pit or circle 10 feet in diameter, 25 yards from throwing position. Each man will throw 6 Grenades, and will be required to place 4 in or close to the pit. A similar test will be made from the prone position—4 Grenades out of 6 to fall in or adjacent to the circle.

INSTRUCTORS' NOTES.

It is important when instructing men with dummy Grenades that all the same precautions should be imposed and explained as would obtain on a live throwing range as follows :—

1. The men should carry out the first safety precaution on all dummy Grenades issued to them.

2. They should be taught to observe the direction of flight of the Grenade for themselves.

3. When practice throwing the men should be arranged in echelon so that those behind do not obstruct or endanger those in front.

4. If the thrower is left-handed the laid-down instructions should be reversed and the pin in the Grenade changed over.

5. Only one man must throw at a time and only on a direct order.

6. Grenades should never be thrown from man to man.

7. No man should attempt to catch a Grenade.

8. No man should pick up a Grenade which has been thrown until ordered to do so.

9. If using dummy igniter sets for priming practice the Grenades must always be de-primed before returning to store.

GRENADE THROWING AREAS.

1. DUMMY GRENADES—HAND GRENADES :

    i. The Hand Grenade in order to be effective must be thrown with accuracy. To teach accuracy under various conditions, a set of simple apparatus for use on the dummy Grenade training course has been designed.

ii. The diagrams Nos. 2—6 show how the apparatus should be laid out. It consists of posts driven into the ground with wire netting to form cages or barriers, over which the Grenade is thrown. Shell holes and distance lines are dug in the ground.

2. LIVE GRENADES—HIGH EXPLOSIVE :

i. The No. 36 Hand Grenade requires a danger area of 300 yards in all directions from any point where it may burst.

ii. It will be noted that the throwing point is inside the danger area. Consequently, special precautions have to be taken. These consist of providing a system of trenches and dug-outs, both for preparing the Grenades and for throwing them.

iii. Diagram No. 17 shows the system of trench-work which provides the greatest safety for live Grenade work. This trench system must be provided on all live Grenade areas.

iv. The diagram actually shows a system with four bays for throwing Hand Grenades. Only one man is allowed actually to throw at a time, and the senior instructor controls all work from a control post. It will be seen at once that this trench system can be halved if desired.

TRAINING WITH LIVE GRENADES.

1. This section deals with training in the use of live Grenades, the safety precautions to be observed are range discipline on the live throwing area. All instructors who are required to handle live material will be taught the preparation of a demolition set and destruction of blinds.

2. Live material will not be used unless a qualified officer or an Army Officer who has qualified at a Small Arms School in the demolition and handling of Grenades or a Home Guard Officer who is in possession of a Certificate signed by the Area Commander, is in charge at all times. The use of improvised Grenades of a dangerous nature, and the carrying out of unauthorised experiments, is forbidden.

3. Demonstrations with live material will not take place inside any building. Dummy material only will be used at lectures.

4. No smoking will take place while live material is being handled.

5. Should a primed Grenade not be expended, the igniter set will be at once removed and returned to its box. Particular care will be taken that no Grenade is returned to store primed.

6. A book will be kept in which the numbers of Grenades, igniter sets and gun-cotton primers drawn from store will be recorded in words and figures ; numbers expended and returned will be similarly recorded, and the totals balanced. Each person taking over the material will sign a receipt in a column or columns which will be provided for this purpose.

7. Steps will be taken to ensure that all concerned with the care, storage or handling of Grenades are familiar with the distinctive markings of live and dummy material, and the rules laid down in the Regulations for Magazines and Care of War Material.

8. Smoke and Signal Grenades will be stored apart from all other material, and will be frequently inspected for signs of leakage or corrosion, especially at the joints of the body. Those showing serious defects of this nature will be destroyed by burning.

9. Gas has a corrosive effect on Grenades. Therefore, in the event of a gas attack, unboxed Grenades should be covered. After the attack is over, the safety pin and working parts should be cleaned and oiled.

THE FIRST SAFETY PRECAUTION.

Whenever a Grenade is first handled, the base plug will always be removed at once to ascertain whether it is primed or not.

1. GENERAL INSTRUCTIONS REGARDING THE THROWING OF LIVE H.E. GRENADES :—

i. Although the use of Grenades can be taught in all its branches by employing dummy material only—the dummy Grenade behaves in exactly the same way as a live one, except that it does not explode—the training of a bomber cannot be considered complete until he has thrown live Grenades.

ii. Live practices are simply to give confidence to the man in handling a weapon which is, wrongly, supposed to be very dangerous. With present-day equipment accidents can generally be traced to one of four main causes :—

> Ignorance.
>
> Negligence.
>
> Deliberate mishandling.
>
> Fright.

The first three can be excluded by training and supervision; the last can be overcome by live practice. Confidence comes quickly after throwing even one Grenade. Should the allowance of Grenades permit, two should be thrown.

iii. GRENADE RANGE. DANGER AREA.—The plan of a live H.E. bombing range is shown in diagram 17. This range is situated in an area which is known as the danger area, and it must be clearly marked out by red flags and look-out men posted whenever the range is in use. A minimum distance of 300 yards must be allowed in all directions from every possible point of burst.

Previously, the danger area for Grenade Ranges was 200 yards from any possible point of burst, as laid down in S.A.T. Vol. 5, 1931.

By A.C. 1 1169, 9.7.41 the distance of 300 yards will be substituted for 200 yards, and all ranges constructed after this date must conform to this new regulation.

On existing Grenade Ranges where the extension of the danger area, owing to the proximity of paths, roads, buildings or other features might lead to the likelihood of persons being outside the 200 yards danger area, but within the new 300 yards danger area, steps must be taken to prevent persons from being within the revised danger area while the ranges are in use.

This range can also be used for firing the Northover Projector with the No. 36 Grenade or A.W. bombs.

iv. TARGETS.—These should be shallow trenches or shell-holes. Targets for throwing will be placed at 20 yards, 25 yards and 30 yards in front of each throwing bay.

The follwing is a sketch showing the danger area for H.E. bombing practice.

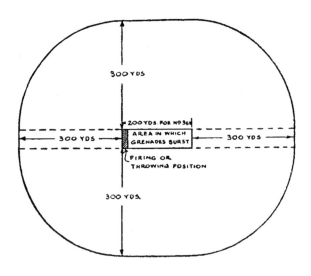

GENERAL POINTS
BEFORE THROWING LIVE GRENADES.

Live Grenades must be carefully inspected as a preliminary to their preparation for use. This inspection is for the purpose of discovering :

i. Defects which might lead to prematures.

22

LIVE GRENADE EMPLACEMENT:

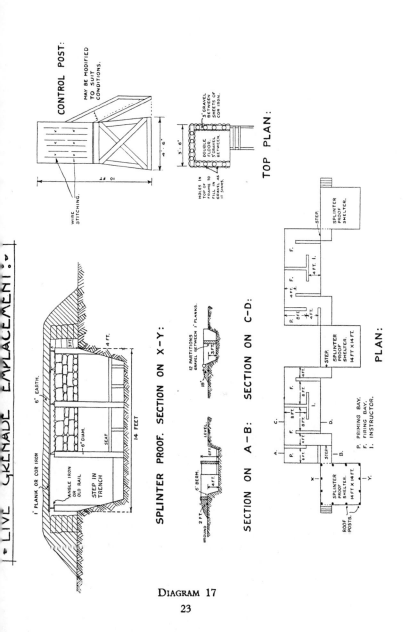

CONTROL POST:

MAY BE MODIFIED TO SUIT CONDITIONS.

WIRE STITCHING.

10 FT

4'-6"

DOUBLE FLOOR 3" GRAVEL BETWEEN.

3"GRAVEL BETWEEN 2 SHEETS OF COR IRON.

HOLES IN TOP OF FRAME TO FILL IN GRAVEL AS IT SINKS.

3'-6"

TOP PLAN:

1" PLANK OR COR IRON

6' EARTH.

3 FT.

4 FT.

ANGLE IRON OR OLD RAIL

6" DIAM.

SEAT

STEP IN TRENCH

14 FEET

SPLINTER PROOF. SECTION ON X-Y:

12 PARTITIONS GRAVEL BETWEEN 1" PLANKS.

18'

3 FT.

LEVEL.

8 FT.

SECTION ON A-B:

6' BERM.

2 FT.

4 FT.

GROUND

SECTION ON C-D:

SPLINTER PROOF SHELTER.

STEP.

14 FT. I.

F.

F.

P.

8 FT.

4 FT.

F.

4 FT.

STEP.

SPLINTER PROOF SHELTER. 14 FT X 14 FT.

F.

4 FT.

I.

F.

8 FT.

8 FT.

C.

D.

A.

P.

6 FT.

4 FT.

F.

STEP.

B.

X

SPLINTER PROOF SHELTER. 14 FT X 14 FT.

ROOF POSTS.

Y.

P. PRIMING BAY. F. FIRING BAY. I. INSTRUCTOR.

PLAN:

DIAGRAM 17

23

ii. Defects which might cause blinds of weak explosions.

Inspection should always be carried out according to a definite plan, in order to prevent points being overlooked. The inspection for H.E. 36 Grenades should be as follows :—

i. The Body :—

(a) Carry out first safety precaution to ensure that the Grenade is safe, i.e., not primed. Examine the outside for cracks through which damp might enter, causing a "blind."

(b) Examine the filling screw to see that it is fully home and sealed to prevent damp entering the charge.

(c) Examine the shoulders to see that they are unbroken so that there can be no premature release of the striker.

ii. The Striker Group :—

(a) Examine the projecting portion of the striker to see that it is properly sealed with luting to prevent damp entering the centre piece, and that the lever is engaged.

(b) Examine the safety pin to see that it is sound and the lever properly held in the shoulders and close to the Grenade to prevent it catching in the ring of another Grenade.

(c) Apply the striker test as follows :—Strip the Grenade, as already taught in first lecture. Take the striker from its spring, remove any grease from the striker and replace striker and spring in the Grenade; see that it works perfectly freely in the striker sleeve.

A Grenade in which the spring appears weak or stiff should not be used.

(d) Examine the centre piece.—Both sleeves should be clean and free from corrosion. Examine the wall between the sleeves for cracks or small holes which would allow the flash from the cap to pass direct to the detonator, which might cause a premature.

(e) Examine the striker face to see that it has nipples and a gas slot.

(f) Re-assemble Grenade as already taught.

iii. The Igniter Set :—

(a) When the igniter sets are inspected they must be held by the cap chamber and fuse. Care must be taken that the detonator is not struck, damaged or subjected to heat or friction. The igniter set is never dismantled.

(b) Examine the central gas escape to see that it is covered with waterproof paper to prevent damp, and is properly fitted to the chamber.

(c) Examine the fuse for firm fixing and varnished joint.

(d) Examine the detonator to see that it is firmly "crimped" to the fuse, and the joint between the fuse and detonator is "luted" to exclude damp.

SAFETY PRECAUTIONS TO BE TAKEN ON A LIVE GRENADE EMPLACEMENT.

The following precautions will be observed :—

i. Before a live practice begins, all danger flags must be raised, look-out men posted, and the whole of the ground, including the danger area, ascertained to be clear of persons and livestock.

ii. A medical orderly provided with all first-aid appliances should be in attendance on the range under suitable cover, generally in one of the splinter-proof shelters. If a medical orderly is not available, a box containing tourniquet, bandages, iodine, etc., must be provided and kept in the observation post throughout the practice. In any case, the medical officer in charge of the troops concerned will be informed that live throwing is to take place.

iii. Every person on the bombing range must wear a steel helmet.

iv. Smoking is forbidden on the range, and at any time when live Grenades, detonators, etc., are being handled or carried.

v. A red danger flag will be kept on the control post during practice. This will be lowered as a signal that practice is about to begin, the Control Officer having first satisfied himself that danger flags and look-out men are in position and that the range is clear. No persons, whether superior officers or otherwise, may enter the danger area whilst the flag on the control post is lowered.

vi. A qualified officer or Army Officer who has qualified at a Small Arms School in the demolition and handling of Grenades or a Home Guard Officer who is in possession of a Certificate signed by the Area Commander will be in charge at all times, and will control the practice from the control post.

vii. An N.C.O., who must be a trained bomber, will be on duty in each priming bay and in each throwing bay.

viii. Not more than one person in addition to the N.C.O. on duty will be in any priming or throwing bay at any time.

ix. Everyone, except the officer in the control post, the N.C.O.s on duty in the priming or throwing bays, and the men actually priming or throwing, will be under cover in the splinter-proof shelters.

x. N.C.O.s in charge of the priming bay and throwing bays are responsible for the throwers' safety, and immediate action must be taken by them if this is in any way endangered.

xi. One N.C.O. will be in charge of the troops in the shelter provided.

xii. No person will leave the shelters for any purpose whatsoever unless the control flag is flying or he is ordered to do so by the Officer in charge.

xiii. No Grenade will be primed until the man enters the priming bay preparatory to throwing. To ensure that this rule is obeyed, the box containing the igniter sets will be in the possession of the N.C.O. on duty in the priming bay, who will issue the number required to each man in turn as he enters and will personally carry out the operation of priming one Grenade; the other Grenade to be primed by the man about to throw.

xiv. No Grenade will be primed or safety split pin withdrawn, and no man will throw without the direct order of the officer in charge.

xv. All movement from the shelter to the range and vice versa will be controlled by whistle or other signal given by the officer in charge.

xvi. Should a blind occur, the officer in charge, and he only, will go out to demolish it, and every blind must be accounted for and destroyed before the party leaves the range.

xvii. Any order to take cover must be instantly obeyed.

xviii. To eliminate any possibility of prematures, all the points laid down for inspection and preparation of Grenades, igniter sets, etc., will be strictly observed.

xix. The "demolition" box must always be on the range during practice.

xx. It is the duty of the officer conducting live practices to foresee the possible incidents that might occur through nervousness, or failure in the material being used, which are likely to endanger those taking part. He should instruct N.C.O.s and men in the immediate action to be followed (see following pages).

GRENADE DROPPED WITH PIN OUT.

It may happen occasionally that a clumsy or nervous man will drop a Grenade when in the act of throwing. In such a case the N.C.O. on duty must be prepared to take such action as may be necessary to ensure safety. No attempt will be made to pick up the Grenade. The occupants of the bay will at once take cover round the traverse, and leave the Grenade to explode. Should a thrower show hesitation or lose his head in such circumstances the N.C.O. on duty must be prepared to act instantly and with energy. He will be the last to leave the bay. This applies equally whether the Grenade has the pin in or out.

METHOD OF CONDUCTING LIVE PRACTICE.

i. On arrival at the live Grenade emplacement each man will hand his live Grenades and igniter sets to the N.C.O.s in charge.

ii. The Control Officer will go through the general points on safety precautions, and each man will clean and inspect his Grenades under the supervision of the Control Officer or qualified N.C.O. In case of suspected flaw, the N.C.O.'s attention will be drawn to the Grenade, and any defective Grenades will be placed on one side.

iii. After cleaning and inspection of Grenades, sections will be told off into details. Each man will take his cleaned but unprimed Grenades and will be marched into the splinter-proof shelter.

iv. N.C.O.s for duty will then take their places; those detailed for the priming bays will have with them the necessary number of igniter sets in their boxes.

v. The officer in charge will take his place in the control post; he will have with him the demolition box and any spare Grenades that there may be. Having ascertained that all safety regulations have been complied with, he will lower the control post flag and order the first detail into the priming bay.

vi. The first detail will prime their Grenades under the supervision of the N.C.O. in charge, and pass on to the throwing bay; the second detail will at once take the place of the first in the priming bay.

vii. Only those Grenades will be primed which are to be used; no man will return to the splinter-proof shelter with a primed Grenade. Should the practice be cancelled for any reason before the number of primed Grenades have been used, the N.C.O.s in throwing or priming bays will see—failing orders to this effect—that the unused Grenades are unprimed; they will retain the igniter sets. This does not refer to the stopping of a practice due to a blind.

viii. When a throwing practice is being carried out the procedure will be as follows :—

Command.	Action.
No. 1 Ready	No. 1 adopts the "Ready" position. The N.C.O. will hold up his hand as a signal to the officer when this has been done to his satisfaction.
No. 1 Prepare to Throw	No. 1 prepares the Grenade for throwing by withdrawing the safety pin and adopting the throwing position with his eyes on or towards the target, and left arm raised, holding the Grenade and lever firmly in the right hand.
No. 1 Throw	No. 1 throws, and observes the direction of flight of the Grenade.
Down	No. 1 and the occupants of all other bays will take cover.

The officer in the control post will observe the actions of the thrower, the direction of flight of the Grenade, and that everyone has taken cover. He will then take cover himself.

After the explosion he will continue as follows :—

Command	
	No. 2 Ready.
	No. 2 Prepare to Throw.
	No. 2 Throw.
	Down.

If there are more than two bays, the procedure will be the same until all have thrown one Grenade. No. 1 will then throw his second Grenade, the same sequence being observed until all Grenades have been thrown by the detail.

Command.	Action.
Detail—Change	First detail moves to its splinter-proof shelter. Second detail replaces first in throwing bays, and third detail moves from splinter-proof shelter to priming bay.

ix. **Action in case of blinds.**—Should a blind occur, everyone will remain under cover until further orders. After an interval of five minutes, the officer in charge will proceed alone to destroy the Grenade where it lies (see Demolition of Blinds).

x. For the purpose of recording and reporting failures and defects, the officer in charge will observe any irregularities in the performance of the Grenades.

REPORTING FAILURES AND DEFECTS.

All cases of failures and defects in material will be recorded, and, if it is considered that they are due to faults in design or manufacture, a report will be made in the prescribed manner.

Such cases would be :—

i. Defects noted during the inspection of Grenades and igniter sets.

ii. Failure of any portion of the igniter sets, e.g., cap, fuse, detonator.

iii. Failure of the Grenade to detonate although the igniter set has functioned perfectly. When this failure occurs, the Grenade is burst into two or three large pieces by the detonator, and, if examined, some of the explosive will usually be found; very little noise is made by a Grenade bursting in this way.

In making such records or reports, the following information will be obtained, if possible :—

Designation of article, number, mark, etc.

Dates of manufacture and packing.

Name of manufacturer, packer's notes, etc.

Any markings on the article in question.

PREPARATION OF DEMOLITION SET AND DESTRUCTION OF BLINDS.

(For Instructors only).

Stores :—

Demolition box containing :—

> Box Fuse, Safety, No. 11.
>
> Box No. 8, Mark VII, detonators.
>
> Cylinder 1 oz. gun-cotton primers.
>
> Luting.
>
> Rectifier.
>
> Pair Pliers.

A knife and matches will be required. The latter will not be carried in the demolition box.

For training purposes the detonators and gun-cotton primers will consist of dummy material.

All officers, warrant officers, and N.C.O.s whose duties require them to deal with live Grenade training must be able to assemble a fuse and detonator and prepare a demolition set. They must know the safety precautions and rules laid down for the conduct of "live" practices and handling of "live" material as set out in the general paragraphs of this section. The Grenade, having been thrown, may sometimes fail to explode. This is called a "blind." When a blind occurs, it is the duty of the officer conducting the practice to destroy it. To do this he uses a demolition set and acts as explained in the following section.

1. Fuses.—In firing charges of explosive, it is necessary for the man who is firing the charge to be able to do so from a safe distance, or to be given time to take cover before the explosion occurs.

For firing charges at a distance, "instantaneous" fuse is employed; this burns at the rate of about 90 feet in one second, and the length used depends on the safety distance required.

i. Instantaneous fuse is never used in Grenade work, even for the destruction of blinds, but it is necessary for everyone who may have to destroy blinds to be familiar with its appearance and characteristics in order to be able to distinguish it. The types of instantaneous fuse in use are as follows :—

> Mark IV. Coloured red. The exterior consists of a waterproof tape covering.
>
> Mark V. Coloured orange, used for training purposes, is ribbed on the outside by means of crossed threads wound round it to enable it to be distinguished by touch in the dark.

Fuse, instantaneous, detonating. — Used for mining and demolition purposes, and is contained in tin or lead tubing.

ii. **Safety fuse** is used in Grenade work in connection with the destruction of blinds, and also forms part of the firing mechanism of Grenades.

It is slow burning, and is used in comparatively short lengths.

The time that elapses between the lighting of the fuse and the explosion allows the firer to get under cover.

iii. **Fuse, safety, No. 11.**—This fuse, coloured black, is used for Grenade-demolition purposes, and burns at the rate of 36 inches in approximately 90 seconds (1 inch in 2½ seconds). There may be a variation of 15 seconds, less or more, in every 36 inches. It consists of a core of finely ground gunpowder surrounded by strands of hemp or jute covered by a layer of gutta percha, and finally by a covering of black waterproof tape. It is packed in tins containing rolls of 48 feet. The rate of burning is marked on the label on the lid of the tin.

2. Fuse precautions :—

i. When a new box is taken into use, the rate of burning should be tested by burning a measured length—say, 12 inches—and noting the time taken and a record placed in the book.

ii. Always unroll the fuse; attempts to straighten out a coil by pulling the loose end will result in the formation of kinks and breakage of the powder trail; this may cause failure in use. The end of the fuse which is to be lighted must be cut on the slant so as to expose a large area of the powder trail.

iii. **Lighting the fuse.**—Fuse may be lighted easily by means of a fusee specially made for this purpose, but generally matches only will be available.

Fuse cannot usually be lighted by applying the flame of an ordinary match; the flame temperature is too low and only results in melting the gutta percha in the fuse, which then covers the surface of the powder trail, and lighting becomes impossible.

The method to be adopted, therefore, is to hold the match against the fuse, so that its head is in direct contact with the end of the powder trail, then to rub the prepared surface of the match-box on the head of the match; the burst of flame in close contact with the powder causes it to ignite at once.

iv. Safety fuse cannot be extinguished even by placing it under water.

3. Detonators.

i. There is one particular property of high explosives which distinguishes them from gunpowder and certain other low explosives; they can be detonated. Detonation is very much more violent than ordinary explosion and, therefore, the effect produced by a given quantity of explosive is very much greater.

Detonation, however, cannot generally be caused by lighting a high explosive in the ordinary way; it is necessary to initiate the detonation in some way, and for this purpose a device called a detonator is employed. Its characteristics are that it can be detonated by a blow (as in a percussion cap), by friction or by a flame. A detonator can, therefore, be set off by the flame from a safety fuse, and, if placed in contact with a high explosive charge, will cause it to detonate.

ii. The detonator, as used in bombing, consists of a small copper tube closed at one end and partly filled with a small quantity of very sensitive and powerful explosive, much too sensitive to be used in large quantities. This explosive is generally Fulminate of Mercury, or some mixture of this substance. These detonators are classified as "service" or "commercial," and their size is expressed by a number.

iii. An example of a service detonator is the No. 8, Mark VII. These are used in bombing, for the destruction of blinds. The No. 8, Mark VII, detonator is painted red and has a small label affixed to it bearing its designation; they are packed in red tin boxes, containing 25, each in a separate recess.

4. Detonator precautions.

In view of the sensitiveness of the explosive contained in detonators, they must be handled with great care. They must not be struck, crushed or bent, nor subjected to heat or friction. No attempt will be made to interfere with the substance contained in them.

They are quickly affected by damp, and should always be kept closed in their boxes.

5. Assembling fuses and detonators.

Cut off the length of fuse required; the end which is to be lighted being cut on the slant and the other end square.

Remove any loose threads that may be sticking to the outside of the fuse where it is to be inserted into the detonator.

Measure the distance from the mouth of the detonator to the surface of the fulminate by inserting a blade of grass, and mark off on the fuse a length $\frac{1}{8}$ inch less than this.

Smooth down the end of the fuse with the fingers, so that it will go easily into the detonator, and insert it gently up to the mark previously made. Do not use a screwing motion in doing this, as the friction which might possibly be caused would be dangerous.

The fuse must now be fixed to the detonator. For this purpose pliers or a jack-knife are used.

Place the pliers over the fuse and slide them down until the jaws are over the mouth of the detonator. Never put the pliers over the filled end of the detonator. Crimp the mouth of the detonator so that the fuse is firmly gripped. A detonator once crimped to a fuse will never be pulled off. Should it be necessary to remove it, the fuse must be cut.

Fuse and detonator are then ready for use, but, to avoid any possibility of flame or water penetrating between the fuse and the detonator, the joint is luted. If no luting is available, clay may be used. Only a very small quantity of luting should be used, just sufficient to fill any small crevices that there may be.

6. Assembling a demolition set.

A suitable length of safety fuse will be fitted to a No. 8, Mark VII, detonator (8 inches of No. 11 fuse gives about 20 seconds). A gun-cotton primer will be prepared for the reception of the detonator by easing out the central hole with the wooden rectifier; this operation must be carried out gently, so as to minimise friction. No metal instrument will ever be used for this purpose. The detonator will then be fitted into the primer; the detonator must never be forced in; if the hole in the primer is not large enough, it must be further enlarged with the rectifier. To prevent the detonator coming out, a little luting should be used to lute the joint.

When preparing the charge, the officer may be assisted by one other person only; with this exception everyone will remain under cover.

7. Method of dealing with blinds :—

i. In most cases it is possible for the Control Officer to deduce the cause of a blind from the moment a Grenade is thrown.

If a cap is fired, the crack is generally audible and indicates that the striker and cap have functioned correctly. If a blind occurs after this indication, and no smoke is seen to come from the Grenade, it means that the fuse is defective.

If smoke comes from the Grenade while it is in the air, or after it has reached the ground, it shows that the fuse is burning properly. If a blind occurs after both these indications, it means that some defect has prevented the flame from reaching the detonator or that the detonator is itself defective.

ii. **Preliminary action of Control Officer.**—When a Grenade fails to explode, the practice will be stopped, and everyone will remain under cover until further orders. An interval of five minutes will be observed from the time the Grenade should have burst before any action is taken to deal with the blind. It is then the duty of the Control Officer to proceed alone to the Grenade, and take the appropriate action as indicated below. **He will not touch the Grenade,** but will immediately destroy it where it lies.

iii. **Destruction of blinds.**—The Control Officer will place the demolition set, as described in 6 above, so that the primer touches the Grenade. In doing so he will take care not to disturb the Grenade. Having ascertained that all other persons are under cover, he will light the fuse and himself take cover. After the explosion he will examine the place, to make certain that the blind has been destroyed.

iv. Whilst engaged in placing or lighting the demolition set, the officer should be careful to fasten his steel helmet or anything likely to fall off and disturb the Grenade.

32